THIS BOOK IS DEDICATED TO

the little kid who's still inside every one of us:

long may you play...

...and to the people in our lives who have let us throw our tantrums,
who have hugged us when we got hurt,
who have reminded us "it's going to be okay",
who have joined us in play,
and who have loved us just for being who we are.

Journey On!

Created by:
Paolina Milana & Joe Edwards
Whitney & Andrew Horton

The tick of the clock seems SLOWER each day

(Although in dog years, I'm a grumpy old stray.)

9 8 7 6 4 3

SOMETHING'S NOT RIGHT.

I can feel it inside.
Sometimes, I wonder

HAS MY SPIRIT DIED?

THIS ISN'T MY LIFE, NOT what I had dreamed.

NO. I had a plan.

I see all my
"FRIENDS"
(most I barely know).
Their posts are so
happy,

yet I feel so
Low.

DID I

take a wrong turn,

at some point
way back there?

Or said **"YES"**
or said **"NO"**

when I meant

I don't care?

Now what I ask...?

SERIOUSLY!

ARE WE THERE YET?

This road's been too long

IS THIS ALL THAT I GET?

I once tried
new things, was
FEARLESS
fun.

Seems so long ago,
when I was
so young.

ARE DAFT LITTLE VOICES and not a big deal,

GIVEN DEMONIC POWERS

and not really real?

Time after time,
I did not
have a clue,
and no guarantee
all my
dreams
would come true.

...like *dancing* past midnight at a Mardi Gras Ball,

singing slightly off key next to Carnegie Ha

What came before
has made me

THIS ME.

I am exactly who

I'm meant to be.

I'll take a
I've learne
there's a worl
right outside
Won't dwe
on the past
I'll jus-
SHIFT INTO
DRIVE

The
journey's
still on!
I'm ready
to fly.

"Oh, the places I'll go"

with no **THERE** to arrive.

I'll **START** my own club. **MEET** somebody new. Dust off my old **DANCE SHOES,** or **WRITE** a haiku.

I'll climb
a new mountain.
Start eating
KALE.
Change this
old channel...
It's my
fairytale!

Enough with those

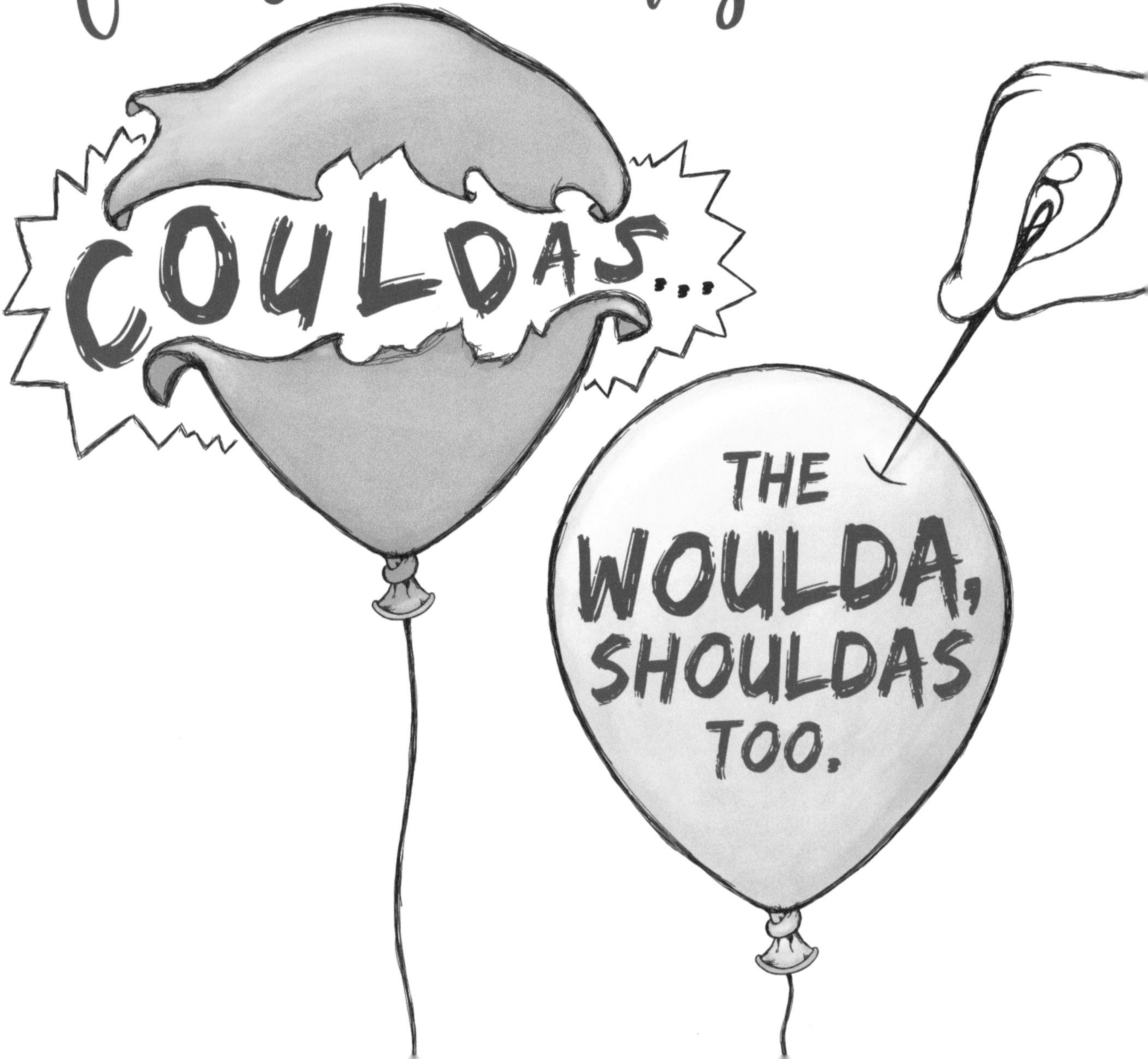

So start down the road;
a new map is in sight.

THERE IS NO WRONG PATH.

...no left fork or right.

The secret's inside
(as you already know).

ONLY YOU can help YOU continue to grow.

Our timing's just right
to go farther than far!

This is Us

The journey of this book "Seriously! Are We There Yet?!" has had us asking th[e] question quite a few times along the way. What we've come to learn, however, [is] that throughout the creative process, we've always been exactly where we we[re] meant to be, and we wouldn't have it any other way. Now knowing that our sto[ry] has found its way to you, we couldn't be happier. We hope it gives you what it's giv[en] to us: A sense of peace, a burst of play, and a reminder of who we really are at t[he] end of every day.

Here's our stories, and how we (and this book) came to be.

WHITNEY & ANDREW HORTON

"Seriously! Are We There Yet?!" was the perfect smack in the face when I first read it. It literally ma[de] me choke up while attempting to read it out loud. Before Paolina came to me with this project, I had b[een] struggling a lot with my own identity as an artist. I was stuck in a vicious cycle of comparison and en[vy] believing that the work I was doing was never good enough. I had started to doubt myself and lose [my] passion for the thing I loved most: My art.

Illustrating this book has broken barriers for me that I didn't ev[en] realize were there. It has helped me, not only because of its words [of] inspiration, but also with the entire creative and collaborative proce[ss]. Before this book, I had convinced myself that my life would never [be] noteworthy unless I made it big in the "art" world. Now I know that tha[t's] a lie. I've already made it big to the people in my life who matter – [my] amazing mom, my inspiring little girl, my encouraging friends, and [my] incredible husband who creatively contributed in so many ways, and who [I] couldn't have done this without.

I hope this book helps prevent people from digging themselves into th[e] same hole I was in, and that through these pages, I can lend them a ha[nd] if they're already in too deep. I've used my love of art in a way that's B[IG] and can only hope that makes a real difference for others. Connect with [me] @HortonDesigns or visit WhitneyHortonDesigns.com.

PAOLINA MILANA & JOSEPH EDWARDS

Originally titled, "Are We The F**k There Yet?!," this book started out a bit of a rant as I battled own "coulda-woulda-shouldas" and struggled to understand how I could be feeling so out of sorts and worthy, despite having succeeded at doing so much. No matter how many "to-dos" I ticked off my list, never was enough. Unceremoniously dismissed and discarded from my job, the one thing that I thought fined me, it only furthered my self-doubts and fears. Now I no longer had a purpose or a plan or even a ycheck, and I didn't seem to belong anywhere. I found myself uncomfortably sitting between what was longer and what was yet to be. So at a time in my life when I expected to hear something similar to GPS proclaiming, "You have arrived"; instead, what rang in my head were the words I whispered to self: "You f**ked up" and "How did you end up here?"

Setting out to get answers and re-imagining this chapter of my story – one that I realized wasn't que to me – I wrote this book. I'm grateful to have found a talented soul in Whitney to bring the aracters to life. And I'm so lucky to have a supportive husband, an engineer by day and a ger-songwriter by night, who lent his lyrical expertise and artistic eye to help make this all that we ped it would be.

This book helped me return to me: That playful kid inside who gets ited at the possibilities of whatever life has in store. It also has made aware of just how far I've come, of my resiliency and reinvention, and of w I've mastered finding the magic in whatever madness I may be in.

This is my wish for you, dear Readers. I hope this inspiring rhyming romp s you remembering who you are and who you've always been, tapping into r own power, loving what is, and knowing there's so much more ahead for a and me. No matter where you're at, the journey is, indeed, still on!

I'd love to know your story, how far you've come and how far you'll go ter reading "Seriously! Are We There Yet?!". Drop me a line at werlina@madnesstomagic.com or connect with me @madness2magic or sit PaolinaMilanaWrites.com.

To get notified of the accompanying workbook,
sign up for the alert at www.madnesstomagic/books.

We want to thank you

...for picking up our book.

We also want to make sure you are on our
VIP mailing list so that you're among the first
to know about the next in our "Seriously!" series.

So skip on over to **MadnessToMagic.com/books**
and grab your FREE poster. It's our gift to you.

And if you love our book as much
as we do, please tell your family and friends
and **leave us a review on Amazon.** We'd be so
grateful to read what you thought.